DAVE'S BOOK OF

AUSSIE DRINKING GAMES

Published in 2022 by OH! Life
An imprint of Welbeck Non-Fiction Limited, part of Welbeck Publishing Group.
Based in London and Sydney.
www.welbeckpublishing.com

Text and Design © Welbeck Non-Fiction Limited 2022
Cover images: ZOO.BY and Gavris Sergey/Shutterstock; other images courtesy Shutterstock.

A CIP catalogue record for this book is available from the British Library.

ISBN: 978-1-83861-130-9

Associate Publisher: Lisa Dyer
Copyeditor: Nicolette Kaponis
Designer: James Pople
Production Controller: Felicity Awdry

Printed and bound in China

10 9 8 7 6 5 4 3 2 1

DAVE'S BOOK OF

AUSSIE
DRINKING
GAMES

OVER 80 GAMES FROM GOON OF FORTUNE TO THONG TOSS

DAVE ANDREW

CONTENTS

INTRODUCTION

Grab your stubby holder, write your address on your arm and prepare to retire some brain cells. It's time to choose your designated driver and get to the bottle-o for some chardy, savvy b, bubbles, bottles, goons, Dapto briefcases, longnecks and

Darwin stubbies. You will need more booze than you can carry because this will be a night to remember ... or not. Stories will be told, legends made and nicknames earned. Drink responsibly, look after each other and may the force be with you.

CHAPTER 1

AUSTRALIA DAY PARTIES

Strike a light! Strewth! You beauty! January 26 is here again. Stock up on Vegemite toast and fairy bread, snags and lamingtons, beer and wine, and don't forget the sunscreen and aspirin. Celebrate this great country with family and friends – we've got a long day ahead!

Goon of Fortune

Think beloved TV gameshow *Wheel of Fortune* without the advertisements and hostesses, and with a lot more fun in the great Aussie outdoors.

Players: Unlimited

You will need: An Australian-made rotary clothesline (aka a Hills Hoist), pegs, a backyard, large goon sack(s) of Aussie wine (the fruitier the better)

Players stand in a circle around the Hills Hoist, at a safe distance. One or more goons of wine are pegged securely to the clothesline. The Hills Hoist is then spun around. When it stops spinning, the person closest to the goon sack must tilt their head back and drink for a specified amount of time.

To win, be the last player standing. Good luck!

Hints & tips: Refusing to drink, excess spillage or leaving the game early all lead to elimination. Add your own rules to make it more fun, such as standing on one leg, or playing in pairs where one person must complete a task before the other can stop drinking.

THONG TOSS

This is a quintessential Aussie DIY, make-it-happen-with-whatever's-close-by attitude that sees footwear become entertainment.

Players: Unlimited

You will need: No equipment other than the thongs you and your mates are probably already wearing and your backyard

Round one: Every participant throws their thongs as far as humanly possible. The longest throw wins. Everyone else drinks.

Round two: A game of finesse and skill, this involves kicking the thong straight off the foot. The longest kick wins, rest of the party drinks.

Round three: Toss at a target. It can be a basketball hoop, bin, open window – anything in sight. Closest to the target wins, everyone else drinks.

Round four: Start variations on different throwing methods. Between the legs, left-handed, blindfolded, discus, shotput, and so on.

BACKYARD CRICKET

Sunshine, a patch of grass, friends, made-up rules, umpiring controversy, walk-offs, walk-ins and drink breaks. Backyard cricket on Australia Day is not so much about the result as about having a go. Aussie! Aussie! Aussie!

Players: Enough for two teams to have an even number

You will need: A wicket (bin, cardboard box), a pitch (indoor hallway, alley, patch of grass, sliver of concrete), a ball (anything from a tennis ball with one side shaved for extra swing to a rolled-up sock), a bat (ideally a cricket bat, but anything from tennis racquets to fence palings can be used), booze

Backyard cricket rules are especially rubbery and dependent on the backyard itself, strength of beer and seriousness of players. Standard rules include six runs and out, tip and run, no outs on the first ball, tree fielders, one-hand-one-bounce and umpiring decisions based on majority rules. At its most basic, though, if batters make a run, they get to nominate a fielder who must drink.

Drink penalties are often levied on fielders who fall over, knock something over, drop a catch, sleep and have food in both hands.

Batsmen can also expect drink penalties for hitting the ball over the fence (added penalties if the neighbour has a dog), losing the ball, damaging windows, breaking the bat and getting caught out.

BOAT RACES

While not always associated with Australia Day, it has been known to happen.

Players: Best for large groups plus a referee

You will need: Beer, beer and more beer

Select teams with equal numbers of players. Then name each team and make a knock-out draw. Teams line up next to each other with a full middy, schooner, stubby, can or whatever beer size has been agreed. At the referee's signal the first player sculls the beer as fast as possible and turns it upside down on top of their head to show it's finished. The second player sculls and so on until one team is finished. Fastest team wins and progresses through to the next round.

Hints & tips: Teams of players can keep track of their progress throughout the day. It is then called a Case Race.

King-of-the-pack Footy

Blast 'Up There Cazaly' on the loudspeaker, slip on your favourite team's guernsey, break out the anti-inflammatory Dencorub and off we go. On Australia Day, there is simply nothing better than enjoying some make-believe footy in the backyard. After a few minutes you will become your favourite player in the Grand Final, marking the footy in front of the goal square after the siren ...

Players: Unlimited

You will need: A good-sized backyard, soft grass, a Sherrin football, booze

The King-of-the-pack player stands at one end of the backyard while the pack of rabid and hard Australian Rules footballers (or your soft, out-of-condition relatives) stand at the other end. The King kicks the ball high so it lands in the middle of the pack where players bravely leap into a tornado of high knees and elbows, fighting to mark the ball above their head. If a mark is taken successfully, that player becomes the King and nominates another player who must take a penalty drink. The King then goes to the end of the garden to again kick the ball high in the air above the waiting pack.

MILK ARROWROOT MAPS

Nibbling at a golden, crunchy biscuit might be its own reward, but there are higher stakes in this game of edible design.

Players: 2–4

You will need: 1–2 packets of milk arrowroot biscuits, drinks

Compete to nibble the best map of Australia from a milk arrowroot without breaking the biscuit.

If your bikkie breaks, you must finish your drink. Drink again if you want another biscuit.

The winner gets to nominate two people to finish their drinks.

Lamington Race

Who would have thought a simple sponge cake dipped in chocolate and coated in desiccated coconut could rise to the heights of a national dessert. No matter how many you have on Australia Day, the calories don't count.

Players: Unlimited plus an independent judge

You will need: Plates, lamingtons, rope, booze

Players are seated at a table with a lamington on a plate in front of them. Everyone's hands are tied behind their backs.

When the judge says, 'Go', the first contestant to finish their lamington is the winner!

The winner then hands out drinking penalties at will.

MIX 'N' MATCH AUSTRALIA DAY CLASSICS

You can mix, match or make up any drinking game today and it will be great fun. There are no rules, except drink Australian Made. No worries, it's world class! Here are some fun ways to compete and enjoy the day the Aussie way.

NAME THE SONG

Playing Triple J's Hottest 100 has become a traditional soundtrack on Australia Day. Instead of just enjoying the tunes, the first person to name the song nominates a sucker to finish their drink.

POOL FLOAT RUMBLE

Time to find a mate with a pool and dust off that inflatable kanga, koala, croc or shark and get ready to rumble.

One-on-one, two-on-two, tag team, kids vs adults – the combinations are endless. Grab a float, jump in and issue the challenge. If you are tossed off the float, you drink. If you toss someone else off, they drink. Any excuse to raise a glass is in good taste today.

Hints & tips: Best-dressed bogan, rock paper scissors or two-up are all excellent excuses to hand out drinking penalties to your friends.

Aussie Aussie Aussie, Oi Oi Oi

You'll most likely hear this chant more times than you can count throughout the day, so make a game of it by drinking every time it comes up.

As soon as anyone yells out 'Aussie Aussie Aussie', all other people at the party must yell out 'Oi Oi Oi' in response.

Anyone who does not respond must have a sip of their beverage.

This is a great way to get people drinking any time there seems to be a bit of a lull in the action, so don't be shy about using it frequently.

CHOCOLATE GAME

When Australia Day is almost over, you are still standing and the only alcohol left in the house is dessert wine, consider the chocolate game just for a laugh.

Players: Those still standing

You will need: Dice, a large block of chocolate, a knife, a fork, Australia Day fancy dress such as a blue singlet, boardies, thongs, a hat with corks, a novelty BBQ apron, ovenproof gloves, zinc, blindfold (optional), booze

A block of chocolate is put on a plate and placed on a table with a knife and fork.

Players roll the dice until someone gets a six. Everyone else must drink while the person who rolled the six must put on the Australia Day fancy dress clothing before attempting to eat the chocolate, a single square at a time, with the knife and fork.

The remaining players roll the dice to get another six and stop the person eating the chocolate. For every square of chocolate eaten, the other players must drink.

CHAPTER 2

COINS & DICE

Search your trackie daks, your flanno, your glad rags, the Kingswood, the tray of the ute, behind the couch or in the clothes dryer. You're going to need some shrapnel because the whole show's a coin toss. Or why not give up your free will to the roll of the dice and let the numbers make a few decisions on how much you should drink. What could go wrong?

AUSSIE COIN FLIP

This is a game played with good friends, a spare evening, a spare bottle of spirits (think rum, bourbon, whisky, gin, vodka) and some spare change.

Players: 2+ and a designated coin spinner

You will need: Shot glasses, a table, a 20-cent coin, booze

There are two ways to play. All players call either heads or tails and the designated spinner flips the coin. If you called it correctly, you don't drink. All incorrect callers must take a shot.

Alternatively, the designated spinner calls AND flips the coin. If the spinner calls it correctly, all other players must take a shot. If the spinner calls it incorrectly, the spinner drinks.

Spinning duties go clockwise around the circle.

Hints & tips: Chasers are allowed by consensus rule.

Quarters

From Woolloomooloo to Wilcannia and beyond, this game is designed to put a bit of a bounce in your step.

Players: Unlimited

You will need: A table with a hard surface, coins, glasses, beer, a strong drink

Place a full beer glass in the centre of the table. If all the players are seasoned professionals, reduce it to a shot glass. Hold a coin between your thumb and forefinger and bounce the coin off the table to land inside the glass. If you shoot and make it, you beauty! You can point at another player and they drink. If you shoot and miss, suffer! The coin passes to the next player. If you hit the rim, you get a free throw.

Hints & tips: Bounce the coin as flat as you can with a slight forward pushing motion. If someone bounces the coin into the glass three times in a row, they get to make a rule that must be followed by all players for the rest of the evening. If you break the rule, you drink.

Chandeliers

Not a trip to view the light fixtures at the Sydney Opera House ballroom, but a game of skill and possibly heavy drinking, which could mean lights out for someone.

Players: Unlimited

You will need: Beer by the carton, a table with a hard surface, glasses, coins

Place a large glass in the middle of the table. Each player pours some of their drink into the large glass. Players place their full glasses around it. One at a time, players attempt to bounce a coin off the table, so it lands in an opponent's glass. If the player succeeds, their opponent must drink. If the player misses, the turn passes to the player on their left.

If a coin lands in the centre glass, everyone must drink.

Hints & tips: Avoid coining your own glass.

DUMMY

For any true-blue Aussie, the chance to have a bet gets our blood pumping. Add the opportunity to drink and make a friend suffer at the same time, and you have an unmissable game.

Players: Unlimited

You will need: Three coins per player, a table, coldies

Players secretly put one, two, three or zero coins in their hand and then hold their clenched fist above a table. Each players makes a guess at the collective number of coins held. Players open their fists and the coins are counted. The player with the closest or correct guess, wins and sits out the remaining rounds. The game begins again, reducing players until there is only one player left, the dummy who has been wrong. Every. Single. Round.

This player must suck down a full drink, plus perform a duty for the group such as shouting a round of drinks, buying chips, telling a decent joke, performing a dare, attempting to get a phone number or paying for a taxi home.

TAPS

Think quick or drink up in this wordless drinking game that can turn a fine mind into a dog's breakfast in short order.

Players: Unlimited

You will need: One coin per player, a table, booze

Players sit around a table with a coin in their hand to 'tap' on the table. One player is chosen to start and play begins in a clockwise direction. Player one taps their coin on the table once. The player to their left then taps their coin on the table once and so on around the circle. The number of taps a player makes determines what happens next. The rules are simple, think UNO by coin taps.

One tap means to continue in the same direction.

Two taps reverses the direction, e.g., to go from clockwise to anticlockwise.

Three taps skips the next player.

If a player misses a tap, hesitates, taps after a reverse or a skip, they must DRINK.

Hints & tips: Going faster makes it harder.

Two-down

Turning the Aussie game of two-up on its head.

Players: A group of mates

You will need: A relaxed, talkative atmosphere, five-cent coins, drinks

Each player has a drink in front of them. Two five-cent coins are held up to show they are in circulation. Players continue to have a chat and a laugh, while being watchful. The coins can be passed from player to player. The aim of the game is to slip a five-cent coin into someone's drink without them noticing. If successful, that person must finish their drink. If two coins are in the same drink, without the player noticing, they must drink a double.

Hints & tips: Guessing the year of the coin in your drink allows you to nominate a second player to down their drink.

Arrogant Bastard

Where are you on the bullshit scale? Whether you have a big hat and no cattle or you are wearing the brown underpants, bring your drinking shoes for this one.

Players: 4–6

You will need: A jug, beer, a coin

Place the empty jug in front of player one. Player one then pours as much of their beer as they dare into the jug. Player one flips the coin and calls it in the air. If they call it correctly, the coin, the jug and its contents pass to the next player. If the call is incorrect, the player must drink the contents of the jug.

ANCHORMAN

This game is part penalty shoot-out, part *Survivor* tribal council and part Shakespearean tragedy. Just when you thought you knew where you stood, you discover the enemy lies within.

Players: Two teams of four

You will need: A table, one coin per player, a jug, beer, a timer

Teams sit at opposite ends of a table with a jug of beer in the centre. Toss a coin to decide which team starts.

Player one from Team A has a single attempt to shoot the coin into the jug. Then player one from Team B shoots the coin and so on until one side has four coins in the jug. The losing team drinks the jug with the players from the losing side deciding how much, or how little, they drink.

The winning team gets to nominate the Anchorman for the losing side. The Anchorman drinks last, finishing what is left in the jug. The Anchorman has two minutes to drink it down.

Hints & tips: Teams can agree on the method of shooting the coin at beginning of the game such as bouncing, a thumb flip or shooting from below table height.

ICE CUBE SURPRISE

It's hot, people are drinking funky drinks so why not join them!

Players: 6–8

You will need: Coins, straws, cocktails, a table, an empty ice-cube tray

Place the empty ice-cube tray in the centre of the table. Players can use their finely tuned Quarters skills to bounce a coin into an empty square of the tray. If the player misses the tray they must sip their drink and try again. Repeat until the player lands the coin in the tray. If the coin lands in an empty cube, the player fills it with their cocktail and their turn is over. If the coin lands in a full cube they must drink whatever is in it.

Hints & tips:
Don't forget the straws.

Dice

Russian Roulette, Wolf Creek Welcome, Broken Hill Bang ... Whatever you call this game, you better put on your big person pants if you want to play. Time to load the chamber, spin the carousel and pull the trigger. This is a game of chance for city and country folk ready to put it all on the line.

Players: 6 plus the dealer

You will need: Cards (ace, 2, 3, 4, 5, 6), a clear spirit, water, shot glasses, dice

The dealer secretly fills six glasses, one with the clear spirit and five with water, and lays out the cards, face up, on the table. A glass is then placed on top of each card.

Players take turns rolling the dice. If a one is rolled, the player must take the shot on top of the ace. If the player rolls a number which has already been taken, they must roll again.

Hints & tips: The dealer must ensure players cannot see the pour. Poker faces and bluffing are encouraged. The dealer can refill the glasses at their discretion.

Left, Right, Centre

Yeah, nah. This game has nothing to do with politics and everything to do with keeping your dough close and your liver functioning.

Players: 4–6

You will need: A table, three coins per player, dice, a large glass, a drink for each player

Place the large glass in the centre of the table. Player one rolls the dice and follows the rules below.

- Roll a one and keep the coin with no drinks given.
- Roll a two and keep the coin with no drinks given.
- Roll a three and pour a sip of your drink into the glass on the table.
- Roll a four and pass a coin to the person on the right who then has to drink.
- Roll a five and pass a coin to the person on the left who then has to drink.
- Roll a six and give up a coin by placing it on the table. Pour as much of your drink as you want in the large glass.

If a player runs out of coins, they must chug the large glass. However, they are not out of the game as someone may pass them a coin. The winner is the player who has the last coin.

TWO DICE

What one dice can do well, two dice can do better.

Players: 4–6

You will need: Two dice, a table, spirits, shot glasses

Players sit around a table and play goes clockwise. Player one rolls the first dice. When rolling the second dice, player one will want to avoid the following, otherwise they must do a shot.

- Rolling a six.
- Rolling a combination that adds up to a six.
- Rolling a double.
- Rolling a double one or a double six.

If the dice is rolled off the table, the player must perform a duty decided by the other players.

Dice are then handed to the next player for play to continue.

Hints & tips: Have bottle of water handy.

CHAPTER 3

TV, MOVIES
& MUSIC

Given the weather Down Under is exceptional (with the odd flood, fire or drought) you would be excused for thinking Aussies never stay indoors long enough to catch an overseas flick. However, we do have electricity and sometimes move away from the campfire long enough to catch a bit of culture.

Of course, we like to combine our viewing with a spot of socialising, a thirst-quenching beverage and a bit of good-humoured banter. So whether you are at the cinema under the stars, the drive-in or in your lounge room, here are some games that are perfect for viewers and drinkers alike.

THE ADVENTURES OF PRISCILLA, QUEEN OF THE DESERT

Time to dust off the sequins and take a ride with two drag queens and a transgender woman as they travel through the Australian Outback. This game is for the true believers. You may need Bundaberg Overproof rum for this.

Every time you hear one of the lines from the list below, simply quaff a shot and put on one of these items: a pant suit, eyeliner, heels, a hat, a feather boa, a corset, flattening straps, glitter, hosiery, a glove, an under bust, a waist cinch.

- 'Great, that's just what this country needs: a cock in a frock on a rock.'
- 'Come on girls, let's go shopping.'
- 'What are you telling me? This is an ABBA turd?'
- 'You can't do that with a ping pong ball?!'
- 'Come on girls, off your snatches. Rehearsal time.'
- 'You've got a face like a cat's arse.'
- 'Oh, shut your face, Felicia.'
- 'Aren't we faaabulous?!'

SHAWSHANK REDEMPTION

While some movies are good enough to watch sober, all movies are more enjoyable with friends and a drink. While there's a good chance you've seen this classic before, rewatch it following the drinking rules below and you and your mates will feel better than ever when the credits roll.

One shot of rum if Hadley:

- Beats or insults someone.
- Kills someone (make it a double).

Drink craft beer if Andy:

- Tells someone he's innocent.
- Says, 'Get busy living or get busy dying'.

Drink an espresso martini if Red:

- Is called by his full name.
- Is at a parole hearing.
- Loses a bet.
- Says the word 'institutionalised'.

Drink ginger beer if Norton:

- Quotes the scriptures.
- Takes a bribe.

Scull a drink if Andy:

- Spins vinyl.
- Tears off his clothes.
- Shines shoe.
- Buys a poster.

PULP FICTION

For those who take their cinema and drinking seriously, this game is for you.

The F-word is said over 250 times in this tale of a boxer, hit men, grifts, murder and foot massages. Choose between eating a Twistie, sipping your brew or going to the toilet every time it's spoken.

Scull when:
- Any character lights up a smoke.
- French fast food is discussed.
- You are confused about the time frame.
- A character uses drugs.

One shot of tequila when:
- You see a bad hairstyle.
- A character plunges a needle into the heart.
- There's dancing.

Drink a full glass of Hunter Valley shiraz on hearing:
- 'In the fifth, your ass goes down.'
- 'Now I wanna dance.'
- 'Did I break your concentration?'

THE CASTLE

This Australian cinematic institution has such iconic lines, they now form the basis of Australia's citizenship test.

Drink spirits every time you hear:

- 'Tell him he's dreamin''
- 'This is going straight to the pool room.'
- 'It's not a house. It's a home.'
- 'Suffer in your jocks.'
- 'How's the serenity? So much serenity.'

Drink Penfolds Grange if you hear:

- 'It's the constitution. It's Mabo. It's justice. It's law. It's the vibe.'
- 'It's the culture, Darryl. The place is full of culture.'
- 'We're going to Bonnie Doon. We're going to Bonnie Doon.'
- 'What do you call this?'

Drink any booze over 12 years old if you hear:

- 'And what law are you basing this argument on?
  The law of bloody common sense!'
- 'Kicking a goal.'
- 'We could just chat for hours.'
- 'A man's home is his castle.'

Forrest Gump

Solid acting. Historic moments. A fridge full of coldies. Simple rules for simple people.

Drink VB, XXXX, Tooheys or Coopers any time a character says:

- 'Forrest'.
- 'Lieutenant Dan'.
- 'Bubba'.
- 'Jenny'.
- 'Mama'.
- 'Alabama'.

Scull if you hear:

- 'Like peas and carrots.'
- 'Medal of honour.'
- 'Most special friend.'
- 'Run like the wind blows.'
- 'Life is like a box of chocolates.'

INDIANA JONES: RAIDERS OF THE LOST ARK

If you want to find treasure, you have to be prepared to dig. Try this game if you have some hard Aussie booze and the Anzac spirit.

Drink a shot when:
- Indiana Jones gets punched.
- The theme music kicks in.

Drink a shot when a character says:
- 'Mr Jones'.
- 'Trust me.'
- 'We have no time.'

Drink a shot plus a beer chaser when:
- Indiana Jones cracks his whip.

MAD MAX: FURY ROAD

A post-apocalyptic desert wasteland with scarce gas and water is the perfect backdrop for drinking alcohol. Better set yourself up for this one because once it starts, you won't be going anywhere.

Drink when you see:

- Blood.
- A smoke signal.
- An explosion.

Drink if you hear the words:

- 'Valhalla'.
- 'War boy'.
- 'Blood bag'.
- 'Furiosa'.
- 'Green Place'.
- 'Witness me'.
- 'Drive'.

Drink doubles when you hear the phrases:

- 'Die historic.'
- 'What a lovely day.'
- 'Hope is a mistake.'

Finish a bottle if:

- Max speaks.

Seinfeld

For a great night in, get on the cans with the show about nothing. Pick your favourite episode and get stuck in.

Sip from your glass if:

- Kramer enters Jerry's apartment.
- Kramer goes to the fridge.
- Someone eats cereal.
- Elaine goes on a date.
- Jerry snogs someone.
- Kramer lights a cigar.
- George's parents argue.
- George gets fired from a job.

Scull a stubby if a character says:

- 'Hello Newman.'
- 'That's a shame.'
- 'Get out.'

Go again if Elaine says it.
Go once more if Elaine says it while pushing someone and they stumble.

Drink a longneck if:

- The camera enters Kramer's apartment.
- George's baldness is mentioned.

FRIENDS

While Manhattan is a long way from Woolgoolga, the universal themes and laughs in this insanely popular sitcom provides endless opportunity to drink with your pals.

Sip an espresso martini if:

- All six characters are in Monica's apartment.
- A Friend is drinking.
- A Friend answers a phone.
- Joey is eating.
- A Friend has a coffee.

Lick, sip, suck tequila if:

- There's a big secret.
- Chandler or Joey is watching *Baywatch*.
- Monica tidies up.
- Ross gets jealous.

Do a Jägerbomb if:

- Monica says, 'I KNOW!'
- Rachel says, 'Noooo.'
- Joey says, 'How you doin'?'
- Janice says, 'Oh. My. God.'

Drink a Death Flip cocktail if:

- A Friend is pregnant or gives birth.
- Joey says something smart.
- A Friend shows up to work.

BABE

A classic Australian film, *Babe* is about a little pig that goes a long way. A little pig goes a lot further, though, with some nice wine and good friends. Put the knife and fork aside and listen carefully for the following drinking prompts.

Sip when:

- There is a voice-over.

Drink when:

- Any animal talks about being eaten.
- The animals argue.
- 'Hoggett' is said.

Finish a drink when:

- Fly says, 'Not as stupid as sheep, mind you. But pigs are definitely stupid.'
- Babe says, 'She called us all "Babe".'
- Ferdinand the duck says, 'Christmas means carnage!'
- Cow says, 'The only way you'll find happiness is to accept that the way things are is the way things are.'
- Cat says, 'Pork they call it, or bacon. They only call them pigs while they're alive.'
- Babe says, 'Move along there ya big buttheads.'
- Ferdinand the duck says, 'Look there's something you should know.'
- Farmer Hoggett says, 'That'll do pig, that'll do.'

GAME OF THRONES

Enjoy a Bundy on the rocks while sitting by the heater watching the drama of Westeros unfold. Stock up on mead, ale or spirits, gather some pals, pick a favourite season and let the drinking games begin!

Take one sip when:

- You hear, 'king in the North', 'winter is coming', 'iron throne', 'milord' or 'milady'.
- A character drinks.
- There is nudity.
- There is any death by arrow, spear or sword.

Take a long draught when:

- A raven's message is read out.
- You hear, 'A Lannister always pays his debts', 'Hodor' or 'dragon'.
- There is a severed body part.
- Varys speaks of his 'little birds'.

Finish a drink when there is:

- Incest.
- A beheading.
- A penis.
- Bran has a vision.

SING, DANCE, DRINK

Drinking and singing go together like bourbon and coke. These classic tunes will get the crowd going if the whole party drinks when they hear these iconic lyrics.

'Thunderstruck' by AC/DC

Better make it just a sip every time you hear 'thunder'. Alternatively, every time you hear 'thunder' you have to scull until you hear the word repeated.

'You're the Voice' by Johnny Farnham

Drink when you hear, 'You're the voice', 'oh', 'whoa' or the sound of bagpipes.

'Working Class Man' by Jimmy Barnes

Drink hard on 'oooh'.

'Can't Get You Out of My Head' by Kylie Minogue

Drink on 'la' until it stops.

'My Happiness' by Powderfinger

Drink on 'I'.

CHAPTER 4

CARD GAMES

It's pissing with rain, there is no sport on, the internet's down, the TV is on the blink and all your mates are about to arrive. Don't fret. No matter where you are, from Bulla Bulla to Bungle Bungle, Curl Curl to Jin Jin, there is sure to be a pack of cards handy. And booze. Whether you want an excuse to get blind, pass some time or just beat your mates ... shuffle 'em up and see what Lady Luck's got in store. Card games are played for money and matchsticks, but the best ones are played for drinks.

Go Fish

Just like you used to play when you were still riding your scooter but with a twist that will have you falling off.

Players: 3–6 plus a dealer

You will need: A deck of cards, drinks

The dealer shuffles the cards and deals five to each player (use as many card packs as necessary). The dealer then places the remaining cards face down in the middle of the circle so that each player can reach. This is the draw pile.

The player to the left of the dealer asks anyone in the circle for a card they already have at least one of. If another player has the card, they must hand it over and don't have to drink. If no one has that card, the group says, 'Go fish', and the player who requested the card must 'fish' a card from the draw pile along with taking a sip, quaff or bottom's up. It is then the next player's turn. The object of the game is to collect as many books (four of a kind) as possible.

SAWTELL SNAP

Sharp reflexes, the cunning of a rat and the ability to drink will give you a fair shake at excelling in this beauty of a game.

Players: A small group works best plus the dealer

You will need: A table where everyone can reach the middle, drinks on the floor, no watches, rings or bracelets

Deal all cards face down, until the pack is finished and every player has an equal number. Don't look at your cards! From the left of the dealer, players go around the circle, placing a card in the centre of the table, only turning it over as it's played.

The first person to play their card says a value starting with 'ace', then the second player says 'two', the third says 'three' and so on all the way up to king, before starting again.

When the number the player says out loud matches the number on the card put down, everyone shouts, 'SNAP' and shoots their hand out onto the top of the pile of cards. The LAST person to do so has to drink and take all the cards from the pile in the middle. The aim is to get rid of all your cards first.

THINK OR DRINK

Mobilise the mouth, wake up your wit and get ready for some hysterical laughter with this mate verse mate challenge.

Players: Unlimited

You will need: A deck of cards, brain cells, booze

Place the deck of cards face down in the middle of the players. Begin with two people, count to three and turn over the top playing card. The two players must think of a word that starts with the same letter as the suit of that card.

For a diamond card, players could shout out, 'DODO', 'DIVA', 'DILL', for example. The player slowest to think of a word loses and must drink.

If you are too smart, or too sober, and find this rule too easy, make it more difficult by naming words that begin with the second letter of the suit, the third letter or even the second-last letter instead.

It all sounds simple until the chardy combines with panic and your pals shout out the weirdest, zaniest, off-beat words which will have you all in stitches.

Hints & tips: Change the pairings and rules to keep the game fresh.

Higher or Lower

This game is for action-orientated players who don't want to sit around on their hands and need something to happen NOW!

Players: 2

You will need: A deck of cards, booze

The dealer flips the top card from the deck. The player must guess whether the next card will be higher or lower than the table card. Simples.

If the player gets it right, the dealer drinks.

If the player is wrong, it's time for them to raise their glass.

Hints & tips: Choose a designated driver early on.

Red & Black

Is your glass half full or half empty? Life's a gamble and this game gives you a 50/50 chance. If you're here for a good time, and not necessarily a long time, this is the game for you.

Players: 2+

You will need: A deck of cards, alcohol

Choose the dealer by drawing cards with the highest card winning. Play then proceeds to the left. Play is between two people at a time, the dealer and a single player. The non-dealer simply guesses whether the turned card will be black or red. The dealer draws the card, and someone drinks! If the player guesses right, the dealer drinks. If the player guesses wrong, then they drink.

Hints & tips: The dealer changes to the left after three players in larger groups.

BULLSHIT

In the Lucky Country, we normally leave the bullshitting to politicians, footy coaches on losing streaks and dodgy mechanics. Now's your chance to get your bluff on.

Players: 2+

You will need: A deck of cards, drinks

Select the dealer, who then deals until every player has an even number of cards. The player to the left of the dealer puts a card, or cards, face down in the middle of the table, which will then become the discard pile. The player then states which cards they have discarded such as, three sevens, a pair of queens and so on. The remaining players must decide if the player in question is telling the truth.

If someone thinks the player has lied, they call 'BULLSHIT!'

The cards in question are the turned over. If they are not as stated, the player must pick up the discarded pile and scull their drink. If the cards are as the player stated, the caller of 'Bullshit' must pick up the cards and scull their drink.

The player that gets rid of all their cards first, wins! Everyone else gets a two-drink penalty.

KINGS

This game puts the gods firmly in control. Let the cards speak.

Players: 4–6

You will need: A deck of cards, booze

All blokes and sheilas sit in a circle around a table or on the floor. In the centre, place a 'penalty' drink glass. Spread a deck of cards face down, with the cards touching each other, to form a chain around the penalty drink. The first player flips a card and must perform an action from the list below.

2 'You'	Point at another player, say 'You', and that person must drink.
3 'Me'	The player who draws the card must drink.
4 'Floor'	Everyone must double tap the floor. The last person to do so must drink.
5 'Guys'	All blokes drink.
6 'Girls'	All sheilas imbibe.
7 'Goal'	Complete the AFL goal umpire's signal for a goal. The last person to do so must drink.

8 'Safe'   Temporary safety. Don't drink.

9 'Rhyme'   The player who drew the card chooses a word. Each player in turn must then select a word to rhyme with it. First long hesitation or failure must drink.

10 'Categories'   The player who drew the card chooses a category and then each player in turn must name something in that category.

Jack   All players must play a round of 'Never have I ever'.

Queen   The player who drew the card must ask the next player a dirty or funny question. That player answers and then questions the next player and so on around the circle. The first player who can't think of or answer a question, must drink.

King   The player who draws the first king picks a spirit, the player who draws the second king chooses the mixer, the player who draws the third king picks the glass size and the player who draws the fourth king drinks and ends the game.

Ace   All players drink and the player who drew the card determines when to stop.

Ten Dead Soldiers

An empty bottle can be a source of pride or despair, satisfaction or longing. This game will have you reaching for an empty like never before.

Players: 4+ plus the dealer

You will need: A deck of cards, empty stubbies (one less than the number of players), drinks

The dealer deals four cards, face down, to each player and places the remaining deck face down in the centre of the table alongside the empty stubbies.

The dealer then takes a card off the top of the pile without showing it to anybody, and decides which four cards to keep and which single card to pass on. The dealer passes their unwanted card to the player on the left. This player must now choose one of their five cards to discard and pass to the next player. When play reaches the last person before the dealer, the unwanted card gets placed in a new pile next to the pile of cards already on the table.

This process continues until one player has either four of a kind or a straight flush. At this point, the player quickly grabs a bottle from the middle of the table and the remaining players must make a play for the other bottles. The loser is the player that is left without a bottle in their hand when the dust settles.

The loser must abide by the dealer's rule which means drinking a glass, a stubby, a shot, a double, a triple ...

RETURN JOURNEY

Returning home after a night out can be the biggest of challenges as you find yourself in unfamiliar terrain with all sorts of hurdles to overcome. Why not stay in and make it easy for yourself?

Players: 2

You will need: A deck of cards, booze, banter

Choose who will be the dealer and who is the person trying to make the return journey. The dealer then lays down a row of six cards, face down, in front of the player trying to get home.

The player making the return journey starts on the left and flips a card. If the card is a non-face card (i.e., a number card) nothing happens. The player has hailed a cab and travels onwards to flip the next card. If the player flips an ace or a face card, they will be issued one or more penalty cards. Think missed the last ferry, a train breaks down or a phone runs out of battery.

Ace   Four penalty cards

King   Three penalty cards

Queen   Two penalty cards

Jack   One penalty card

For each penalty card that is issued, the player must take a shot, sip or scull of their drink. That's right, ace is four penalty cards and four drinks. When the player has successfully drunk their way through all the cards dealt, they have made the return journey.

Hints & tips: If the dealer runs out of cards, simply reshuffle the cards already played.

UNO Drinking Game

If friends have dropped by with a bottle and you have a pack of UNO, combine the two for an excellent night in.

Players: 4–6

You will need: A deck of UNO cards, spirits, agreed glass size

Deal seven cards to each player with the remaining cards forming a draw pile in centre of table. Play UNO as normal but action cards now become drinking cards. Additional drinking rules as follows:

• For every card drawn, a sip must be taken.
• When the direction is reversed, the player who misses
  a go must drink.
• If you are skipped, you must drink.
• If you receive a 'take two' card, take two sips or pass it on if you are able.
• If you receive a 'take four' card, take four sips or pass it on if you are able.
• If you forget the rules or ask a question, take one drink.
• If you forget to shout UNO on your last card, finish drink.
• If you play a wild card, designate a player to finish your drink.
• If you have the most cards left at the end of the game,
  finish the bottle.

The winner is the first person to get rid of all their cards.

FUCK THE DEALER

Yes! It really is as simple as that. Nothing gives more satisfaction than stitching up your mates, and of course nothing gives them more happiness than returning the favour. This is a game of intuition and luck.

Players: 2+

You will need: A deck of cards, drinks, balls of steel

Players form a circle and each draws a card from the pack. The player with the lowest card is the dealer and the player to the left of the dealer becomes the 'high roller' for the round.

The high roller pours a drink 'wager' and places it between themselves and the dealer. The sky is the limit. The dealer then draws three cards and places them face down. The high roller then tries to guess something about each of the three cards, for example the suit of the first card, the exact value of the second card and if the third card is higher or lower than the second card.

If the high roller fails in each of the three guesses, they must drink. If the high roller has guessed one or two answers correctly, the dealer must drink.

KILLER

We all have moments when we might want to knock off someone we know. Release some tension with this friendly game of cards instead. *Wink*

Players: 4–10

You will need: A deck of playing cards, eyes in the back of your head, drinks

Before you begin, take out cards from the deck so that the deck has only one red card, the ace of spades and enough black numerical cards so that every player receives a card and there are none left over. For example, if there are six players, the deck should have one red card, the ace of spades and four black numerical cards.

Choose a player to shuffle the cards and deal. The player dealt the red card is the 'killer'. The player dealt the ace of spades is the 'detective'. The rest of the players dealt black numerical cards are the 'civilians'.

The killer must then 'wink' at a player to kill them without being noticed by the other players. When a player 'dies', they must say, 'I'm dead', scull their drink and leave the game.

The detective must figure out who the killer is before all the civilians die. If the detective accuses a person of being the killer and is incorrect, the detective must drink. If the accused is the killer, they must drink.

Hints & tips: A ten-person game can be played with two killers and two detectives. The detective can be given two or more guesses.

F-YOU, PYRAMID

You might be closer to Cairns than Cairo but that doesn't mean you can't enjoy this game of the ancients. This is a fun way of getting other players to suck the raw prawn.

Players: 3+ plus the dealer

You will need: A deck of cards with jokers removed, a table, alcohol, cups

The dealer places cards in a 4-3-2-1 'pyramid' formation, face down, on the table and the remaining cards are dealt out equally to the players. The dealer flips over the card at the bottom corner of the pyramid and counts down five to one. Players then have five seconds to place a card on top of it.

Only cards of the same suit or number can be played.

The first player to place their card down says, 'F-you' to another player. If that player has a card of the same number or suit, they play it and say, 'F-you' to another player. If that player has a card of the same number or suit, they play it.

If the player can't, or doesn't, play a card, they must drink. As the players progress up the pyramid the drinking penalties increase as follows:

• One drink for cards in the bottom row.
• Two drinks for cards in the second row.
• Three drinks for cards in the third row.
• Four drinks for cards in the top row.

The aim of the game is to discard all your cards, avoid drinking and nominate a sucker to drink.

Hints & tips: Each player can keep their cards as long as they want. They can choose whether to accept a drink penalty and keep a card for later or play their card.

SCREW YOUR NEIGHBOUR

Bringing your mates down-to-earth is a time-honoured tradition Down Under. There is no better way to do it than passing them a dud card during a friendly game and watching their face. At least they can have a cool drink to soften the blow.

Players: 3+ plus the dealer

You will need: A deck of cards, booze

The dealer gives each player one card. The player to the left of the dealer goes first. This player looks at their card and must choose whether to swap their card with the player on their left, or to pass, with the aim of the game to have the highest card by the end of the round. The second player then makes a choice to keep their card or swap it with the player on their left and so on.

Any player with a king on the initial deal must flip it face upwards. The player to the right of the king cannot swap and is stuck with their card. (Aces are low, kings are high.)

The dealer chooses whether to keep their card or swap it from the top of the deck. At the end of the round players flip their cards and the one with the lowest card must drink.

CHAPTER 5

HEN & BUCKS PARTIES

You have kissed frogs, dodged some wombats, wusses and wankers. Maybe you have dumped dud roots, drop kicks and fruit loops and finally lassoed the colt or filly of your dreams. Who wouldn't want to celebrate after all that effort?

Whether you have one night or a weekend to celebrate with your posse, it's just a question of how much fun you really want to have. Here are a few ideas to get the party started.

FOUR QUEENS

This is the game to decide almost anything. It often starts as the who, what, where and how of drinks but by the end of the night has been known to decide a first child's name, bridal hairstyle, honeymoon activities, fates and futures. Trust in the cards.

Players: Entire party

You will need: A deck of cards, booze

The dealer deals cards to each player until there are no cards left.

Queen/king of hearts picks the type of drink.

Queen/king of diamonds orders the drink.

Queen/king of spades pays for the drink.

Queen/king of clubs drinks the drink!

Repeat and change up each queen or king's duties.

Hints & tips: Variations are unlimited and can include, queen/king of hearts picks a tattoo image, queen/king of diamonds picks the body location, queen/king of spades pays and queen/king of clubs gets it!

Guess Who

Everyone has a secret and there is nothing like a special occasion, some great friends and a few drinks to let your guard down. Friendships will be strengthened, classified information revealed and vows of silence sworn with this fun game.

Players: Entire party

You will need: Notepads, pens, a hat, shot glasses, good booze

Each player writes a secret about themselves onto a piece of paper, folds it and places it inside a hat. Player one picks a secret from the hat, reads it aloud and then must guess who the shame belongs to.

If the player guesses correctly, the person whose secret it is must own up and down their shot. If the player guesses wrong, they have to down the shot.

Two Truths & a Lie

They say a little white lie doesn't hurt. But we all know a great big fat one is much more fun!

Players: Entire hen party

You will need: Booze, glasses, a more than a bit of chutzpah

Players take it in turns to face the group and tell two truths and a lie. The rest of the group must put their heads together and work out which one is the lie. If the group gets it right, the liar takes a shot, scull or slurp. If the group gets it wrong, then they must all have a shot, scull or slurp.

CONFESSIONS OF
A BRIDESMAID

What could be more fun than poking around in the collective cupboard of a bride and her besties? If you think there may be some skeletons in amongst the shoes and little black dresses, this is the game for you.

Players: Entire hen party

You will need: Alcohol of any flavour, enquiring minds, memories of past indiscretions

Begin with the player seated to the left of the bride-to-be. Player one poses a single question on any topic to the player seated next to them. The question must begin with, 'Have you ever ... ', with the aim of getting player two to confess to an embarrassing deed. Player two must only answer, 'Yes' or 'No'. If the answer is 'Yes', player two must drink. If the answer is 'No', player one must drink. Player two then asks a question to the player seated next to them and so on.

BEER/PROSECCO PONG

A fun game of skill and luck, just add bubbles or hops.

Players: Two teams of six

You will need: A table, 12 glasses, two ping pong balls, straight aim

Rack six glasses into a triangle formation at each end of the table. Fill the glasses with beer or prosecco. Teams take turns bouncing a ping pong ball so it lands in one of the opposing team's glasses. If the ball goes in, then your opponent must drink the contents of the glass and remove it from the table. The game is won when one team has no glasses left on their end of the table.

Play-Doh Pictionary

The perfect game for mixing art, imagination and booze – all against the clock.

Players: Entire party

You will need: Paper, pen, a hat, a tub of Play-Doh, imagination, crafts skills, quick fingers, booze

The best man/woman must write down various objects on slips of paper, which are then folded and placed in a hat. Players are then split into two teams. A player from each team is chosen and picks a slip of paper from the hat with an object written on it. They must then fashion the object out of Play-Doh as quickly as possible for their team to guess. The first team to guess correctly wins a point.

All players in the losing team must drink!

Hints & tips: Objects are limited only by your imagination and can include: a ball and chain, a body part, a ring, a rose, a baby, the Sydney Harbour Bridge, the Sydney Opera House.

Banned Words

It can be hard keeping your trap shut …

Players: Entire party

You will need: Brain cells, drinks

At the beginning of the night, all players must agree on a handful of words to never be mentioned throughout the evening. They could be related to the wedding, or the bride/groom, partners or the night itself.

Whenever any of these words are accidentally said, the forgetful player is given a choice of a drink or a challenge.

Hints & tips: Challenges can include, hugging a bouncer, getting a phone number and so on.

MOST LIKELY TO ...

Time to take a walk down the hall of mirrors and find out about your reputation.

Players: Entire party

You will need: Drinks

Players sit in a circle with their drinks in front of them. The player to the left of the bride/groom is player one and asks a question to the group starting with, 'Who is the most likely to ...'. The whole group counts down to one, then points at the player most likely to do that thing. The person with the most fingers pointed at them must scull their drink.

Hints & tips: Alternatively, each player must take a sip for every finger pointed at them. Questions can include, 'Who is the most likely to have sex at the wedding/own a cattle station/pole dance with a prop snake?' and so on.

DRINK IF ...

The perfect game to get everyone to let their hair down.

Players: Entire party

You will need: A pen, paper, booze, glasses, honesty, laughter, no judgement

Appoint one wicked player the ceremonial head and have them write a series of probing, risqué questions on a piece of paper, starting with 'Drink if ...'

The ceremonial head then asks each player in turn a 'Drink if ...' question. If the player has done the deed, they must drink. Questions are continued to be asked until all players have pleaded guilty or fallen off their chair.

Hints & tips: Example questions can include, 'Drink if you've ever kissed a rugby league player', 'Drink if you've never seen a red-back spider', 'Drink if you don't know the population of Australia', 'Drink if you've got an embarrassing photo on your phone' or 'Drink if you've heard anyone here having sex through the walls.'

Mr & Mrs Questions

This game is the party's last chance to put the bride on the spot. Drill down and find out everything, from who wears the pants, to bad habits and best body parts.

Players: Entire hen party

You will need: A pen, paper, booze, organisation

Before the party night, have the groom-to-be answer a series of questions. On the night of the party, these same questions are asked of the bride-to-be. If she gives the same answer as the groom the rest of the party must drink. If the bride gives a different answer to the groom, the bride drinks.

Hints & tips: Example questions can include, 'Would your partner rather have sex or watch the Grand Final?', 'Partner's holiday choice: Outback or Gold Coast?' or 'Who would your partner rather be, the Prime Minister or a movie star?'.

CHAPTER 6

SPORTS

Blessed with sunshine, fresh air and wide-open spaces, it's no wonder Down Under loves its sport. After a day of honest toil, Aussies come together to sip refreshing beverages and gather in tribes to watch teams in combat. But if the primal urge to compete surges through you, drinking games can be added to the sporting mix so you can assert dominance, fulfil tribal allegiance and just have some fun!

NRL DRINKING GAME

Coaches, counsellors, teachers, prison warders ... they all say we need structure. So here it is. Rather than drink willy-nilly as you watch the match, here is a game to bring discipline to your boozing. The only guidelines are to choose the beverage of your choice, don't watch the game alone and wait for the whistle.

Sip when there is:

- Some push and shove.
- A completed set of six.
- A line drop-out.
- A penalty.

Scull when there is a:

- Charge down.
- Scuffle.
- Penalty goal.
- Try.
- Sideline conversion.
- Serious knee injury.

Do a shot when:

- A player is sin-binned.
- A player is sent off.
- A player is knocked out.
- A player is stretchered off.
- There is an intercept try.
- There is a 20-point lead.
- There is a falcon.
- There is a video ref balls-up.
- There is a one-on-one strip.
- There is an exposed buttock.

AFL Drinking Game

A fair dinkum, contact Aussie sport created in Victoria in 1858, played by 18 players on an oval field with four goal posts at each end across four, 20-minute quarters. Pace yourself for this one.

Sip amber fluid of choice when there is a:
- Hit out.
- Handball.
- Mark.
- Push and shove.

Double sip when there is a(n):
- Behind.
- Inside 50.
- Intercept.
- Contested mark.
- Melee.
- Free kick.
- Out-on-the-full.

Scull when (there is a):

- 50m penalty.
- Goal.
- A fight breaks out and the bench empties.
- Streaker.
- A footy hits the post.
- Coach loses it.
- Star player gets flattened behind play.

Drink schooner of spirits if:

- It's a draw.
- The commentator quotes the Bible.

Every time a star player goes up for a mark, the last person to put their hands in the air must do a shoey.

SOCCER DRINKING GAME

It's only fair you get a chance to drink when enjoying the world's most popular game. Given Australians come from all over (and travel all over) teams from Korea to Columbia, Canada to Kazakhstan enjoy our support. Whether you are cheering for your team with pints of bitter, shots of soju, aguardiente or a caipirinha, this is the game for you.

One drink when there is a(n):

- Free kick.
- Throw in.
- Corner.
- Offside call.
- First goal.
- Player dive.
- Substitution.

Two drinks when there is a:

- Second goal.
- Yellow card.
- Goalkeeper save.

Three drinks when there is a:

- Red card.
- Third goal for one team.

One drink when the commentator says:

- 'Football is a funny old game.'
- 'He gave 100 per cent.'
- 'A game of two halves.'
- 'At the end of the day.'
- 'How did he miss that?'
- 'Couldn't fault them on effort.'

Sip when a manager says:

- 'One game at a time.'
- 'There are no easy games at this level.'

Drink a glass of water:

- Every time the referee gets screen time.
- If there is a real injury.

One drink when there is/are:

- Flares.
- A pitch invasion.
- A laser on the goalkeeper or penalty taker.

One penalty drink for slow games when there is a:

- Shot off target.
- Shot on target.
- VAR check.
- A player ruled offside.

If the game is defensive, slow or boring, get the stopwatch and someone must scull a beer for every five minutes when nothing happens.

At end of game players must be pissed enough to swap shirts. If anyone is worried a shirt won't fit, or doesn't match their pants, there is a three-beer penalty.

Cricket Drinking Game

A game played with just a bat and ball and that can end in a draw despite going for five days? Sounds silly. But it's also one of Straya's most popular pastimes. Combine it with drinking and you are onto a winner. Given the length of a cricket match varies from five days to 200 balls, you'll need to adapt the rules to suit, but let's say it's a 50-over one-dayer.

Scoring shot	Sip.
4 boundary	Sip.
6 boundary	Double sip.
6 over bowler's head	Shot.
Maiden over	Shot.
Fall of wicket	Drink rest of glass.
Dropped catch	Host provides more food.
Unsuccessful appeal	Drink a glass of water.

Batsman recalled for overstepping	Double sip.
Bowler completes allotted overs	Drink rest of glass.
Ducks	Shot.
Batsman scores 50	Double sip.
Batsman scores 100	Triple sip.
More than 20 off the over	Finish glass.
100 on debut	Triple sip.
Dismissed on 99	Drink a glass of water.
Hat trick	Double sip.
Five wickets	Triple sip.

Toilet breaks allowed only on lbw, boundary rope catch, successful review.

BASKETBALL DRINKING GAME

A basketball game is not that long. This game should not be attempted by amateur level drinkers, or those with plans for the next day.

Pick a side and drink whenever your team:

- Misses a lay-up.
- Misses a dunk.
- Misses a free throw.
- Calls a time out.
- Gets pinged for a foul.
- Shoots an air ball.

Two drinks if:

- A player from your side fouls out.
- A player from the other sided performs a double-double.

Three drinks:

• If an opposition player performs a triple-double.
• For a buzzer beater from the opposing side.

Everyone must drink when:

• Scores are tied.
• A scuffle breaks out.
• Someone puts up 15 points in a quarter.

Opposing players must drink when:

• A 3-pointer is scored.
• A dunk is scored.

Rugby Union Drinking Game

Simply pick a side and strap yourself in.

Drink when the following are scored:

Penalty goal	One drink.
Try	Two drinks.
Conversion	One drink.
Penalty try	Three drinks.
Drop goal	One drink.
Match-winning drop goal	Three drinks.
World-Cup winning drop goal	Unlimited.

Bonus point drink awarded if:

• A try is scored from over halfway.

• A goal is scored from over halfway.

• The referee is knocked over.

• There are tears during the anthem.

• There is a red card given to the opposition.

Sip for:

- Kick-offs.
- Lineouts.
- Knock-ons.

Drinking penalty.
Do not drink for five minutes if:

- There are more than two scrum re-sets in a row.
- There is a high tackle debate.

Drink anytime the commentators say:

- 'Through the phases'.
- 'Earn the right'.
- 'Play in the right areas'.

Drink if the post-match player
interview contains the words:

- 'Process'.
- 'Lessons'.
- 'Got the result'.
- 'The boys'.

CHAPTER 7

WORD GAMES

The right word at the right time can uplift, challenge, heal and inspire. It could also get you out of a speeding fine or into a promotion. In these games, the right word can help you get out alive. Be on your toes and you will be sweet, while your pals are left holding the rough end of the pineapple.

SENTENCES

Strike me pink! Wish you had paid more attention in English? No worries! You can still thrive in this game with some imagination, the odd conjunction and your gift of the gab.

Players: Unlimited

You will need: Booze, vocal cords

Players stand in a circle and someone is picked to go first. Player one beings by shouting out a random word. The player to their left adds a word that forms a sentence without finishing it. Play continues around the circle until someone hesitates too long, creates a sentence that doesn't make sense, is the third person to add an adjective or finishes the sentence. The loser must pay a heavy drink penalty before play starts again.

Hints & tips: Words like 'and', 'but' and 'if' can become boring and repetitive so try limiting or banning them, or add a drinking levy for their use. An example could be, player one says, 'Politicians', player two says, 'are', player three says 'useless', player four says, 'bastards'. Player four accidentally ended the sentence so must drink.

Animals

From kookaburras to black cockatoos, barking frogs to chooks, you possums will be spoilt for choice in this ripper drinking lark.

Players: 5+

You will need: Drinks, imagination, acting chops

Players stand in a circle and choose and perform a funny animal noise and action for the group.

One player is picked to begin. Player one performs their animal noise and action, then the noise and action of another player. The player that corresponds to that noise and action, performs the noise and action of the first player, their own noise and action and the noise and action of another player. Play then passes to this new player and continues. Hesitation or mistakes incur a severe drinking penalty.

Hints & tips: Anyone who laughs or does not perform with gusto must take a drink.

Invisible Ball

Sometimes the best fun happens over nothing at all, but you better concentrate otherwise you might find yourself as useless as screen door on a submarine in under ten minutes.

Players: 5+

You will need: Beer, bubbles or a box wine of your choice

Players stand in a circle holding a drink. Someone is elected to start and indicates left or right as the invisible ball's direction of travel. The ball's movement is directed by three words. 'Whizz' means the ball passes to the next player, 'Bounce' means the ball skips over the next player and lands with the following player and 'Boing' means the ball changes direction. Think acoustic UNO.

The first player then starts the game by saying one of the three words. Whichever player the ball is passed to, replies with a further command dictating the ball's movement. If any player hesitates or makes a mistake, they must drink. The last correct player, or the player who has had nothing to drink, re-starts the ball's movement.

PISSED AS

We've all done the action, now say the word. This quick word game will end in a mouthful for someone.

To play, gather some mates and a large drink each, and go around the group, simply saying a word for 'drunk' from the hundreds that exist. Once you start, they will roll off the tongue.

Here are a few to get you in the mood: blind, tipsy, hammered, legless, trolleyed, rotten, smashed, maggoted, plastered, wasted, gooned, sauced, sloshed.

Alternatively, use phrases like: oiled-up, rat-arsed, shit-faced, gut full of piss, full as a goog, the wobbly boot, three sheets to the wind, drunk as a lord.

Hesitate, capitulate, make a mistake? Drink up or shout the clubhouse.

HANDS UP, HANDS DOWN

Handballing a footy is fun, but this game of handball is way serious.

Players: 6+

You will need: A solid table, a bottle top, a timer, booze

Players are split into two teams of three or more and sit at opposite ends of a long table. A team leader is selected for both sides. The players in Team A hold their hands open above the table at chest height. The leader of Team A holds a bottle top in the air so it is visible to both teams.

The leader of Team B then says, 'Hands down!' and Team A put their hands underneath the table. Team A now have 30 seconds to pass the bottle top along (or not), trying to deceive the other team.

When time is up, the leader of Team B says, 'Hands up!' and Team A must bring up their hands, fists clenched, above the table to chest height.

The leader of Team B calls, 'Hands down!' again and Team A slam their hands palm down on the table, yelling 'Ha!' at the same time. (This veils the sound of the bottle top hitting the table.)

Team B must now guess which hand has the bottle top. If the hand Team B picks holds the bottle top, Team A must drink. If the hand is empty, Team B must drink.

Hints & tips: If playing in large groups, more than one guess can be given.

WOULD YOU RATHER?

A naughty game that will have you between a rock and a hard place with Buckley's chance of getting out. Either reputation or sobriety will be lost. Possibly both.

Players: 5+ (the more the merrier)

You will need: Booze

Player one begins by posing a question to the group beginning with, 'Would you rather ...?' Questions can include, 'Would you rather a boxer's nose or trucker's gut?' or 'Would you rather your partner be unfaithful or have a permanent scar on your face?'

Player one then counts down from three and says, 'Show!' All other players 'show' either one finger (first option) or two fingers (second option). Players who vote for the least popular option must drink.

As, Bs & Cs

Any galah knows the alphabet. You may be able to talk under wet cement, but if you can't come up with a word on the spot, please enjoy your drink!

Players: 4+

You will need: Alcohol, words

A player starts by selecting a category – the sky's the limit. The player to their right then picks something within that category that begins with the letter 'a'. For example, someone starts by choosing 'fruit' as a category and the second player could say 'apple'. The third player could say 'blackberry' and so on. So far so good until someone hesitates or makes a mistake. Then harsh drinking penalties must be applied.

The player with the last correct answer gets to choose a new category.

What the Fuck?

The world's most useful word is at it again. This game is one-part christening, one-part tribal drumming, the rest is booze.

Players: 6+

You will need: Drinks, a table

Players sit in a circle around a table and have fun giving each player the most appropriate 'fuck' name. For example, Dud fuck, Sneaky fuck, Dirty fuck, Blonde fuck, Short fuck. Players must then remember everyone's 'fuck' name. There are no reminders during the game so study hard.

The game starts with all players slapping the table and clapping the rhythm to 'We Will Rock You' by Queen. Player one then chants their own name, then says, 'What the fuck?', then says, 'Can I get a ...', then says the name of another player.

Here it is in slow motion, 'Blonde fuck, what the fuck? Can I get a ... Sneaky fuck?'

From there it's simple. Continue as above. Mess up and you must drink up.

Hints & tips: Speed up the rhythm to make the game harder.

FUZZY DUCK

A fun tongue-twister and brain-basher to get the party started, or finish it off completely. You have been warned.

Players: Unlimited

You will need: Booze, your wits

Players sit around a table or in a circle. Some brave soul starts the game by saying 'Fuzzy duck'. The player to their left has a choice. They can repeat the phrase 'Fuzzy duck', and play continues in the same direction to the next player on the left. Or they can ask, 'Duzzy?' ('Does he?'). This changes the direction of play, and the phrase to 'Ducky fuzz'.

Now play goes back in the direction it came, with players having to repeat the new phrase. Every time someone says 'Duzzy?', the direction and phrase changes.

Hesitation, saying the incorrect phrase or speaking out of sequence all incur a drinking penalty. A referee may be required.

CHAPTER 8

CELEBRITY
& CULTURE
DOWN UNDER

Straya is home to a lot more than king brown snakes, red-back spiders and hungry crocodiles. We've got talented artists and musos, king makers and film makers, a big country and even bigger attractions. Time to see how much you know about the land Down Under.

CELEBRITY SURNAMES

From Hoges to Rusty, Nicole to Kate, Heath to Hugo, there's no shortage of famous Aussie names to choose from for this star-studded game.

Players: Unlimited

You will need: Local knowledge, booze

Player one calls out the name of an Australian celebrity. The player to their right must think of another celebrity whose first name starts with the first letter of the previous celebrity's surname. For example:

Player one picks Joel Edgerton.

Player two picks Eric Bana.

Player three picks Ben Mendelsohn.

Player four picks Margot Robbie.

Mistakes, hesitation and repetition all require a penalty drink.

Hints & tips: An alliterative surname (think Janis Joplin, Courtney Cox, Sharon Stone) means the direction of play is reversed and all other players drink.

Celebrity Forehead

Think Kylie, Michael, Barnsey, Cathy, Wally. Think sport, music, stage or TV. It's right there on the tip of your tongue, or rather stuck on your forehead.

Players: Unlimited

You will need: Post-it notes, pens, drinks

Players secretly write down the name of a famous person on a Post-it note and adhere it to the forehead of the player to their right without them seeing it. In a clockwise direction, players take it in turns to ask 'Yes' or 'No' questions about the celebrity on their forehead.

If a player receive a 'Yes' to their question, they may ask another. Otherwise, they must drink and play passes to the next player.

The last player to guess their identity must drink and shout the table. If they do not guess their identity, they receive an extra drink penalty.

ACTOR & MOVIE

Remember the time you watched *The Castle* rather than taking Bluey for a walk? Turns out it was an investment, not an act of laziness, that is about to pay off with this homage to films and film stars.

Players: Unlimited

You will need: Brain cells, drinks, a set time limit

Pick a player to begin and then proceed clockwise around the circle. Player one calls out the name of an actor, for example, 'Michael Catton'. Player two then says the name of a movie the actor appeared in, for example, *'The Castle'*. Proceed around the group until a player cannot name a movie with that actor, within the agreed time limit. That player then must quaff the drink penalty.

Alternatively, if a player can name a movie the actor did not appear in within five seconds, they get a pass. The other players get a minute to think of other movies the actor has appeared in and if they get to four movies, the player receives an additional drink penalty. Or, the player must perform a duty for the group for every other film the group names.

The last correct player gets to call out a new actor's name to start the next round.

CODE OF CONDUCT

Combine the love Australians have for nicknames and their distrust of politicians and you have the next game.

Players: Unlimited

You will need: A master of ceremonies, paper and pencil for each player, drinks

The master of ceremonies must read from the list below of prime ministerial nicknames. Players must match as many nicknames to real names as they can.

Nicknames	Prime Ministers
Liar from the Shire	Scott Morrison
Mr Harbourside Mansion	Malcolm Turnbull
Mad Monk	Tony Abbott
Ju-liar	Julia Gillard
Milky Bar Kid	Kevin Rudd
Honest John	John Howard
The Mortician	Paul Keating
Silver Bodgie	Bob Hawke
The Prefect	Malcolm Fraser
The Young Brolga	Gough Whitlam

After all ten nicknames have been read out, cards can be swapped amongst players and marked.

If a player receives a perfect score, everyone else must drink a double.

For the player who receives the highest score, everyone else drinks a single.

For the player who receives the lowest score, they must stop drinking.

SIZE MATTERS

No matter how you slice it, it's nice to stand out from the pack.

Players: Unlimited, plus one responsible adult

You will need: Paper and pen for all players, booze

Players list numbers 1–14 on their sheet of paper and create two columns.

In the form of a question, the responsible adult reads out the names of attractions from the list below and players must name the town and state in which it belongs. For example, 'In what town and state can the Big Prawn be found?'

Attraction	Location
The BIG Prawn	Ballina, NSW
The BIG Pineapple	Woombye, QLD
The BIG Potato	Robertson, NSW
The BIG Lobster	Kingston, SA
The BIG Koala	Dadswells Bridge, VIC
The BIG Banana	Coffs Harbour, NSW

The BIG Easel	Emerald, QLD
The BIG Merino	Goulburn, NSW
The BIG Rocking Horse	Gumeracha, SA
The BIG Golden Guitar	Tamworth, NSW
The BIG Mango	Bowen, QLD
The BIG Boxing Croc	Humpty Doo, NT
The BIG Ram	Wagin, WA
The BIG Bogan	Nyngan, NSW

Players can either score a point per question, with incorrect answers receiving a one drink penalty, or answers can be totalled at the end. Players can score one point for each correct answer, with a maximum score of 28.

If a player scores below 14, they must drink a double. If a player gets all towns correct, every other player must drink. If a player gets all states correct, every other player must drink. If a player gets all answers correct, everyone else must drink doubles.

The highest score is the winner and everyone else drinks.

AUSSIE CULTURE 101

This is not rocket science, but if you're not on your game, you're going to the moon.

Players: 6+ (the more the merrier), plus a compere

You will need: Paper and pen for each player, drinks

The compere reads from the list of trivia questions below and players must write down their answers. After every question, the correct answer will be are read aloud and any players who are incorrect must drink.

Which character said, 'That's not a knife. That's a knife!'?
Mick Dundee

Which character said, 'There's a smell in here that will outlast religion.'?
Kenny

Which singer wants to get physical?
Olivia Newton-John

Which actor played Wolverine?
Hugh Jackman

Which actor played Lionel Logue, the man who helped King George VI to speak?
Geoffrey Rush

Which actor played Galadriel?
Cate Blanchett

Name the actor who played Thor.

Chris Hemsworth

Finish the sentence: In like _ _ _ _ _.

Flynn

Which country singer is the hubby of Tom's ex?

Keith Urban

Who was the Crocodile Hunter?

Steve Irwin

Which movie includes the line, 'Tell him he's dreaming'?

The Castle

Complete the line, 'You're terrible _ _ _ _ _ _'.

Muriel

Which movie includes the line, 'That'll do pig, that'll do.'

Babe

Which movie includes the line, 'Sometimes you pick your dog. Sometimes your dog picks you.'
Red Dog

Which movie includes the line, 'Fish are friends not food.'
Finding Nemo

Which character said, 'Why would I shoot a bloke BANG, then carry him to the bloody car and whizz him off to the hospital at a hundred miles an hour? It defeats the purpose of having shot him in the first place. What's more, it's bloody insulting!'
Chopper

If a player gets all questions right, everyone else must drink.

If a player gets fewer than five correct, they must stop drinking.

STRAYA POP QUIZ DRINKING GAME

Time to saddle up for this fun game which can decide historical bragging rights and the evening's drinking duties.

Players: Unlimited, plus a compere

You will need: Paper and pen for each player, booze, brain cells

Answers are marked at the end of each question.

Name the infamous armour-wearing bushranger.
Ned Kelly

Which year was the Sydney Harbour Bridge finished?
1932

'Crotch rocket' is Aussie slang for ... ?
A motorbike

What is another name for a sheepskin boot?
Ugg

What is a Bondi cigar?
A number two floating in the ocean

What is Australia's national floral emblem?
Golden wattle

Can dingoes bark?
Yes

Who was the architect of the Sydney Opera House?
Jørn Utzon

When was federation in Australia?

1 January 1901

Which state invented the pie floater?

South Australia

How many species of the world's most venomous snakes live in Australia?

21

Which Australian state produces the most wine?

South Australia

Name Australia's biggest art prize.

The Archibald Prize

Which Australian Prime Minister entered the Guinness Book of Records in 1954 by sculling 2.5 pints in 11 seconds?

Bob Hawke

Which sporting trophy is the smallest?

The Ashes urn

True or False: Australia was the second country in the world to give women the vote.

True

What is the ratio of sheep to person in Australia?

6:1   There are over 150 million sheep in Oz.

What is a Bushman's alarm clock?

The Kookaburra's laughter

Which is larger, the Great Wall of China or the Australian Dingo Fence?

The Dingo Fence is 5,600km long, three times the length of the Great Wall of China.

If a player answers any question incorrectly, they must drink.

If a player answers fewer than ten questions correctly, they must stop drinking.

If a player answers all questions correctly, everyone else must drink.

Ozstraya Citizenship Drinking Game

Time to saddle up for this fun game which can decide historical bragging rights and the evenings drinking duties.

Players: Unlimited, plus the host

You will need: Paper and pen for each player, booze

The host, that's you reading, asks the player on the left the first question. If that person knows the answer, they say it loud and proud. If the answer is correct, that player makes everyone else drink. If the answer is incorrect, they must drink a double. If the player is unsure of the answer, they can pass but must take a penalty drink. The next person has the same choices. If it goes round the whole table and nobody can answer correctly, everybody must remove an item of clothing.

What is a Greenie?
VB

How many millilitres in a pony?
140

What is a Dapto briefcase?
Cask wine

How many millilitres in a jug?
1,140

What is cardboardeaux?

Red wine from cask

What is a brownie?
Bottle of beer

How many millilitres in a Darwin stubby?
2,250

What is an Anzac shandy?
Mix of beer and bubbles

What is a cleanskin?
Wine bottle without a label

What does the phrase, 'I'm dryer than a Pommy's bathmat' mean?
Let's drink

SPORTING QUIZ DRINKING GAME

All those hours of watching sport and listening to your partner rabbit on about their favourite team is about to pay off.

Players: Unlimited, plus a referee

You will need: Pens, paper, timer, booze

Divide players into two teams and nominate captains. Captains are in charge of writing down the answers. Only written answers are counted. The referee then asks Team A the first question. If they answer correctly, then Team B must drink. If Team A is incorrect, they must drink. If the team isn't sure of the answer, they can pass to Team B.

Which male tennis player won the Grand Slam in 1962 and 1969?

Rod Laver

Which female tennis player won 24 Grand Slam women's singles titles?

Margaret Court

Which male cricket player is regarded as the greatest batsman of all time?

Donald Bradman

Which Australian distance runner lit the Olympic cauldron for the 1956 Olympics?

Ron Clarke

Who is the most successful Bathurst 1000 driver?

Peter Brock

How many times did Makybe Diva win the Melbourne Cup?

Three

Which Australians have the following nicknames?

'Gidget'	Layne Beachley
'Pup'	Michael Clarke
'Junior'	Wayne Pearce
'Madame Butterfly'	Susie O'Neill
'Big Dell'	Wendell Sailor
'The Body'	Elle Macpherson
'The Shark'	Greg Norman
'SOS'	Stephen Silvagni

Which Aussie national teams have the following nicknames?

Dingoes	Men's Ultimate Frisbee
The Irukandji	Surfing

Aussie Stingers	Women's Water Polo
Diamonds	Women's Netball
Pearls	Women's Rugby Sevens
Steelers	Men's Softball

Teams receive these lightning round questions at the same time and have two minutes to answer.

List the winners of the last five Brownlow medals.

List as many NRL teams as you can.

List as many AFL teams as you can.

List as many Melbourne Cup winners as you can.

Hints & tips: No phones please.

AUSSIE DRINKING TOASTS

1. Bottom's Up

2. Cheers Mate

3. Call: Cheers Big Ears
Response: Same Goes Big Nose

4. Raise a Glass

5. Scull

6. Down the Hatch

AUSSIE DRINKING TERMS

Tide's Gone Out
Glass needs refilling

Liquid Lunch
Afternoon meal consisting of drinks only

Beer O'clock
End of any workday/Friday afternoon/Any time

Adam's Ale
Water

Frothy
Beer

Coldie
Beer

TA FOR READING!

Beauty! Onya! Ripper! Pearler! Bonza!

Just making it to the end of the night can be hard enuf. Making it to the last page of a book on drinking games is quite a thing. Hope you've made some new friends and had a great time.

I raise my glass to you and wish you well.